D0575608

# OLIPHANT:
# An Informal

*Also by Pat Oliphant*

FOUR MORE YEARS
THE OLIPHANT BOOK

# Gathering

by

Pat Oliphant

Simon and Schuster · New York

Copyright © 1978 by Pat Oliphant
All rights reserved
including the right of reproduction
in whole or in part in any form
Published by Simon and Schuster
A Division of Gulf & Western Corporation
Simon & Schuster Building
Rockefeller Center
1230 Avenue of the Americas
New York, New York 10020

Manufactured in the United States of America
1 2 3 4 5 6 7 8 9 10

Library of Congress Cataloging in Publication Data

Oliphant, Pat, date.
An informal gathering.

1. American wit and humor, Pictorial. I. Title.
NC1429.043A4 1978 741.5'973 78-6501
ISBN 0-671-24031-5

*The early drawings in this book appeared originally in the* Denver Post, *copyright © 1973, 1974, 1975 by the Denver Post–Los Angeles Times Syndicate. The balance of the drawings appeared originally in the* Washington Star, *copyright © 1975, 1976, 1977 by the Washington Star–Los Angeles Times Syndicate. The Oliphant cartoon is distributed exclusively throughout the world by the Los Angeles Times Syndicate.*

# OLIPHANT:
# An Informal Gathering

1/24/73

*Lyndon Baines Johnson is dead.*

1/26/73

*The Vietnam War is at an end . . .*

2/12/73

**WELCOME BACK**

*. . . and the troops start coming home.*

2/18/73

NIXON SAVES
ECONOMIC OPPORTUNITY MISSION
CLOSED
SOUP & SERVICES
DEFENSE CONTRACTORS
I'M A (SLURP) NIXON FREAK!

3/24/73

**"THIS STUFF IS BARELY FIT FOR DOGMEAT! BY THE WAY, WHERE *IS* . . . THE . . . DOG . . . ?"**

*Food costs—the astronomical is countered by the unimaginable inedible.*

3/25/73



*Dickie still has a grip on things . . .*

3/27/73

**". . . THE TRUTH IS, I'M IN DIRE NEED OF A BLESSING!"**

*. . . but a sense of nervousness prevails.*

4/10/73

**"I WAS ALWAYS THANKFUL HE WASN'T A POLITICAL CARTOONIST!"**

*Meanwhile, all the good guys are dying.*

4/19/73

**"BY GOLLY!" CRIED DICK, AS HE SWUNG TO SAFETY, "SOMEONE WILL PAY DEARLY FOR THIS!"**

*However, Dickie has not yet begun to fight. Blame, yes. Fight? . . . That comes later.*

5/31/73

**SECURITY BLANKET**

*And if blame fails, one can always hide behind the obvious.*

7/25/73

**"WE WERE ONLY OBEYING ORDERS! . . ."**

*The Watergate hearings are televised to an embarrassed nation and to the world. John D. Ehrlichman, top Nixon aide, manages to personify that administration's arrogant philosophy of "Might Is Right."*

7/10/73

7/29/73

**APPROVED BY GOOD WHITE HOUSE-KEEPING**

*Another great arrogance—the bombing of Cambodia.*

8/14/73

**EYEBALL TO EYEBALL . . . SORT OF**

*Nixon refuses to comply with the subpoena for nine tape recordings issued by Watergate special prosecutor Archibald Cox.*

11/2/73

11/20/73

ALL OF THE PEOPLE ALL OF THE TIME? ER, NO... SOME OF THE PEOPLE ALL OF THE TIME?.. ER, NO... HOW ABOUT 39% OF THE PEOPLE 98% OF THE TIME?.. ER...
..AND THERE'S YOUR PLACE IN THE HISTORY BOOKS!

11/23/73

**"I CAN NAME ONE BUSINESS THAT'LL BITE THE DUST IF HE BANS SUNDAY DRIVING!"**

*A country-wide fuel shortage looms, and Nixon proposes measures to save the nation's energy.*

**11/28/73**

**"MISS WOODS, MOST BOSSES WOULD HURL YOU OUT ON YOUR EAR FOR WHAT YOU'VE DONE, BUT . . ."**

*When the famous Watergate tapes of Oval Office conversations are played, a mysterious gap shows up. Nixon's loyal secretary, Rose Mary Woods, claims an accidental erasure has occurred while she was transcribing the tapes.*

**12/11/73**

*President Nixon shows us he is land-poor.*

7/18/73

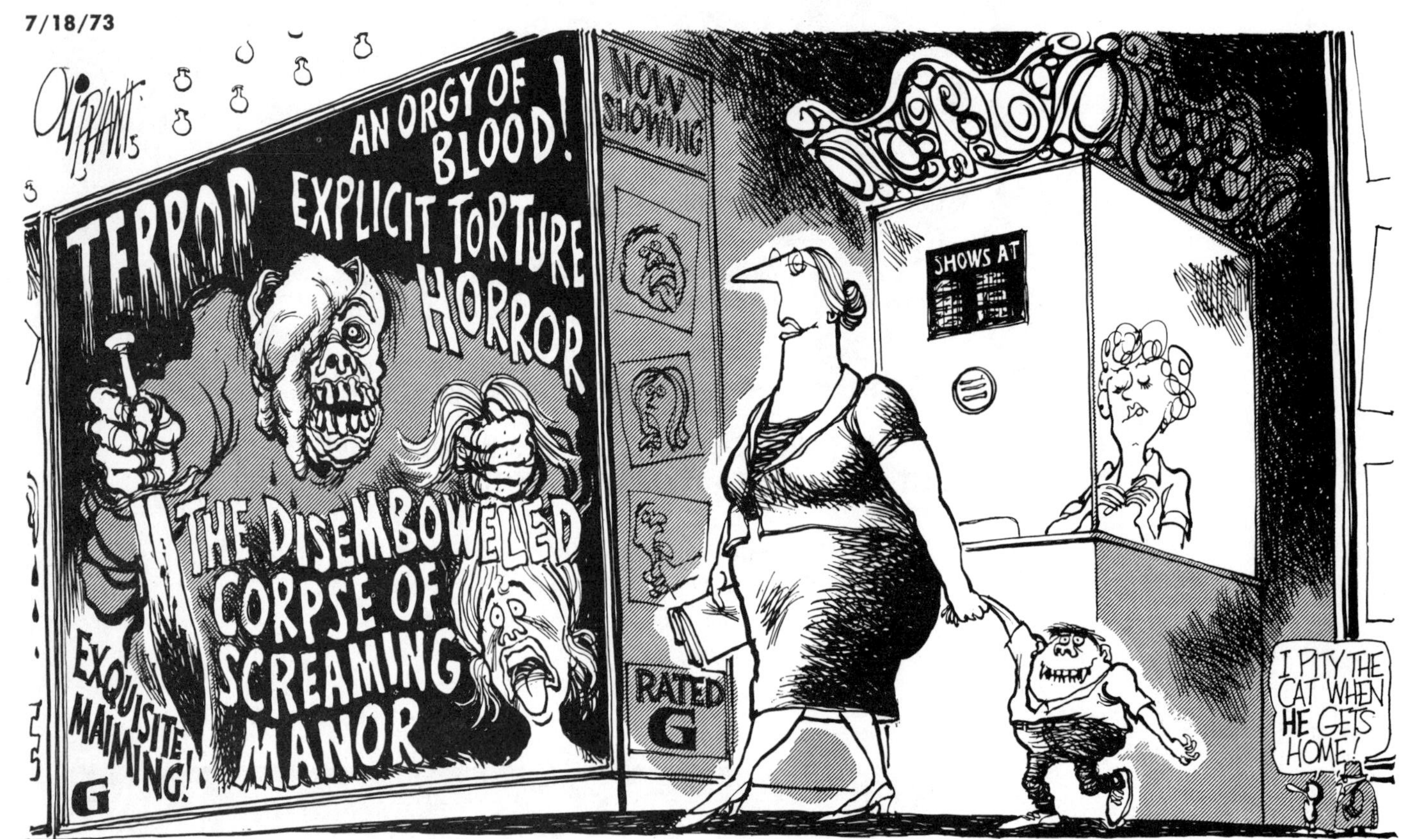


**"AT LAST, A MOVIE WITHOUT ALL THOSE FILTHY SEX SCENES!"**

*Against this backdrop, how can children be harmed by seeing G-rated movies?*

1/3/74

**"AREN'T YOU THE JOKER WITH THE ENEMIES LIST? . . .
WHAT AN UNEXPECTED PLEASURE!"**

*President Nixon, the IRS claims, owes $450,000 on his 1969 to 1972 tax returns.*

1/6/74

*Happily, there are other diversions for the beleaguered Dickie . . .*

1/17/74

*However . . .*

2/1/74

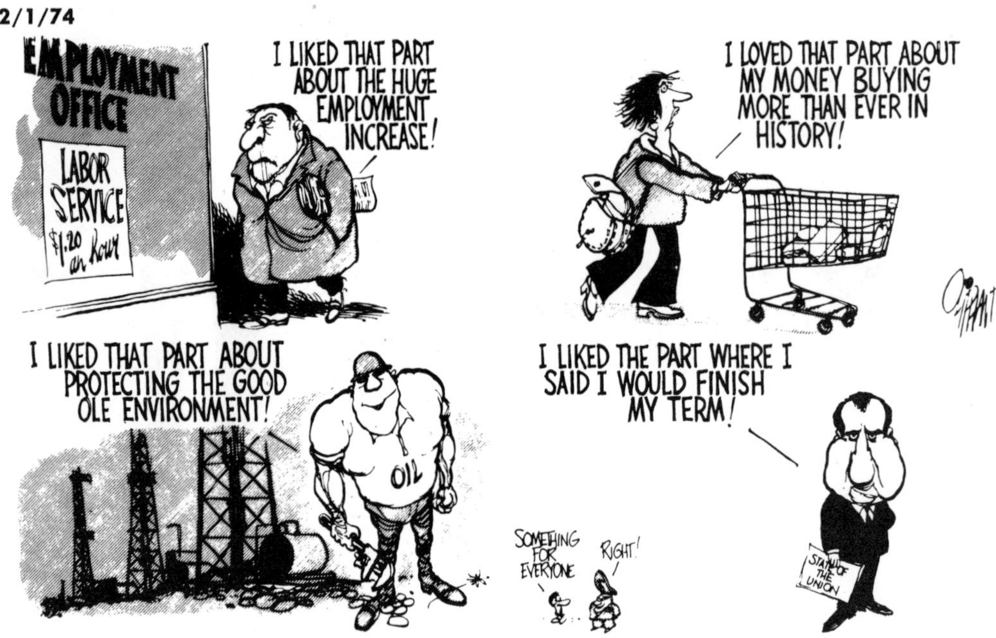


*But if nothing else works, let's have an optimistic State of the Union message.*

1/11/74

*Damn the environment—full speed ahead!*

2/14/74

**TRIUMPH**

*Another arrogant regime, this one in Russia, is also having trouble with the free expression of ideas. Alexander Solzhenitsyn is banished.*

4/24/74

**"PICK UP YOUR CHECKS AT THE REAR DOOR— THIS ENTRANCE IS FOR REAL VETERANS!"**

*Who said old soldiers fade away . . . ?*

5/5/74

**"OF COURSE HE CAN'T READ OR WRITE— HE'S SPENT MOST OF HIS LIFE ON A BUS!"**

*He can always learn to read in college.*

5/17/74

**"I WISH WE COULD HAVE MET UNDER DIFFERENT CIRCUMSTANCES . . ."**

5/21/74

INDIA JOINS THE NUCLEAR CLUB

6/21/74

"I'M FROM THE AMERICAN CIVIL LIBERTIES UNION, AND WE'VE HAD A COMPLAINT . . ."

*The ACLU, in its wisdom, upholds the idea that exclusively all-male activities like Little League baseball would induce hair on the palms and well deserved—therefore, all such activities should include girls . . . or some such reasoning.*

7/18/74

"IT COULD BE WORSE—WE COULD BE IN CYPRUS
TRYING TO KEEP A BUNCH OF GREEKS AND TURKS APART!"

7/21/74

**"I WISH I COULD SHARE YOUR OPTIMISM, JIM, BUT TO ME IT ALL LOOKS RATHER HOPELESS— THE NFL WILL NEVER SETTLE THIS STRIKE BY FALL!"**

*James St. Clair, ace lawyer, is engaged to assist Richard Nixon, ace football coach, with his defense. And when it comes to politics and football, Nixon always has his priorities in order.*

7/28/74

**"BE RIGHT WITH YOU, LEON—RIGHT THIS SECOND . . . AFTER I SORT OUT A FEW THINGS HERE."**

*Watergate prosecutor Leon Jaworski waits with growing impatience for the Nixon tapes.*

8/7/74

"I DIDN'T KNOW IT WAS LOADED!"

8/8/74

*Vice President Gerald Ford waits to assume the presidency.*

8/9/74

*Nixon resigns.*

8/27/74

**"C'MON, HEALTH, HEALTH, HEALTH! LET'S GET THE OL' CIRCULATION MOVING AGAIN!. . ."**

*Ford hauls an atrophied Congress into action again.*

8/26/74

**"TRAFFIC AT THREE O'CLOCK . . . AND I GUESS WE WON'T EVER SEE THE LIKES OF HIM AGAIN!"**

*Charles Lindbergh dies.*

8/30/74

*Nixon is pardoned . . .*

9/1/74

**LOOKING FOR TREES**

*. . . and is granted incredible transition expenses.*

10/4/74

**"JERRY, ABOUT YOUR PROPOSED UPPER-INCOME SURTAX . . . WILL THAT APPLY TO MY $55,000 PENSION OR MY $200,000 TRANSITION ALLOWANCE?"**

*An attack of phlebitis keeps Nixon confined to San Clemente. The raised foot becomes a symbol of his unwillingness to return to Washington to testify any further in the Watergate matter.*

10/23/74

**"DOC, MY CONDITION IS AGGRAVATED BY PINING FOR MY RECORDS AND TAPES IN WASHINGTON . . . COULD YOU WRITE ME A PRESCRIPTION FOR THEM?"**

10/11/74

**"NOW WE COME TO THE OFFICES OF THE HOUSE WAYS AND MEANS COMMITTEE, HEADED BY . . ."**

*Meanwhile, Wilbur Mills keeps the Washington circus going by performing strange antics with a stripper named Fanne Fox.*

11/3/74

**"HURRY IT UP, WILL YOU, NOAH?"**

*Gerald Ford is faced with keeping things together for the Republicans.*

11/21/74

**"OH HIM? . . . WELL, HECK, WE ONLY TURN HIM LOOSE WHEN IT'S NECESSARY!"**

*The FBI has been keeping some strange pets.*

12/13/74

**"DEAR PRESIDENT FORD, WE ARE DELIGHTED TO HEAR THAT THE COUNTRY IS NOT IN A FINANCIAL CRISIS. PROMISE YOU'LL LET US KNOW WHEN IT IS. YOURS TRULY . . ."**

*The economy decays. Old people are reported to be eating dog food. President Ford remains optimistic.*

12/20/74

**"ANOTHER LOAD OF OLD FOLKS—WHERE DO YOU WANT 'EM?"**

*Stories are surfacing of lamentable conditions in the nation's nursing homes.*

12/27/74

"GOOD GRIEF, ARE WE STILL MESSING WITH NERVE GAS?
—DON'T ANSWER THAT!"

1/2/75

**"YOU'RE ANGUISHED!!!"**

*The Watergate conspirators Haldeman, Ehrlichman, Mitchell and Mardian are sentenced to prison terms for their part in the offense. Their old boss expressed his reaction as "anguish."*

1/30/75

**"VERY WELL, BARRY . . . I'LL COME BACK!
BUT THIS TIME WE DO IT *MY* WAY—NO MORE MR. NICE GUY!!"**

*Barry Goldwater visits and talks with Nixon at San Clemente.*

1/31/75

**". . . WITH HIS LECTURE THIS EVENING, 'HOW TO MAKE A FORTUNE FROM YOUR COUNTRY'S MISFORTUNE,' MAY I PRESENT MR. JOHN DEAN."**

*Watergate wasn't a complete loss for everyone.*

**1/23/75**

**"OF COURSE I BROUGHT THEM WITH ME—HOW DO YOU THINK I GOT IN HERE?"**

*FBI Director J. Edgar Hoover has been promoted to the Great Agency in the Sky, but his files are missing . . .*

**2/2/75**

*Signs of an economy in deep trouble.*

2/20/75

"HELP!"

4/11/75

**"SHE'S THE RIGHT HEIGHT, SHE'S FEMALE AND SHE'S CAUCASIAN—BUT PATTY HEARST SHE AIN'T!"**

*Heiress Patty Hearst, kidnappee turned urban guerrilla, remained an elusive target for the FBI.*

4/15/75

**"CONGRATULATIONS, YOU HAVE QUALIFIED FOR A REBATE! BUT FIRST A FEW QUESTIONS ABOUT YOUR POLITICAL AFFILIATIONS, SEX LIVES AND DRINKING HABITS . . ."**

*Just a few more questions from the good old IRS.*

4/23/75

*Henry Fishinger is not held in the highest esteem at this time by some of the nation's allies.*

4/24/75

4/29/75

**"SO, FINE, HE'S GOING TO GET TIRED . . .
WHEN IS HE GOING TO GET TIRED??"**

5/23/75

**"LISTEN! I'M PLAYIN' OUR SONG!"**

*With election year coming closer, George Wallace begins some well-known solos.*

5/26/75

**"THEY SAY SOMEBODY JUST ROBBED THE JOINT . . ."**

*Congressmen have a great sense of timing.*

5/27/75

*Cambodian gunboats seized the U.S. merchant ship* Mayaguez *in the Gulf of Thailand. President Ford, needing a prestige boost, reacted mightily with military action. Seeking to avoid protest to this, the Pentagon delayed release of the American casualty figures (5 dead, 16 missing, 49 wounded).*

5/19/75

**"AHH, YES! A MAN HAS TO BELIEVE IN SOMETHING, AND I BELIEVE I'LL HAVE ANOTHER DRINK!"**

*Vietnam, Cambodia, the* Mayaguez*—it's enough to make a lush out of anyone.*

8/14/75

**"I HAVEN'T BEEN ABLE TO DRILL THEM
SINCE THEY VOLUNTEERED FOR YOUR CRAZY DRUG TESTS!"**

*A retired U.S. Army general reveals that the CIA, with the Defense Department's blessings, conducted secret LSD drug tests on Army personnel in the 1950s.*

7/9/75

**"DON'T WORRY ABOUT A LITTLE PREGNANCY, LIEUTENANT— WE NO LONGER DISCRIMINATE AGAINST SUCH THINGS— AND THAT'S ALL I WANT TO HEAR ABOUT IT, SERGEANT!"**

9/17/75

**"I WAS THINKING OF ENLISTING— BUT, THEN HE WINKED AT ME!"**

5/30/75

**"WE CAME HERE TO REASSURE YOU OF OUR DEPENDABILITY—
ER, WOULD YOU PLEASE DO THE SAME THING FOR US?"**

*President Ford and Henry Kissinger at large in Europe.*

2/27/75

**"WE COULD NATIONALIZE IT, OR MAYBE GET SOME ARAB TO BUY IT—BUT WHERE COULD YOU FIND AN ARAB THAT DUMB?"**

6/1/75

**"IT'S A DEAL, THEN—I SELL YOU THE BRIDGE FOR FIVE MILLION BUCKS, AND FOR TEN BUCKS EXTRA I THROW IN THE ENTIRE CITY OF NEW YORK!"**

6/4/75

"OUT! THE INTEGRATION DOESN'T EXTEND THIS FAR!"

4/28/75

**"YES? . . ."**

6/10/75

**"DO NOT LEAVE GUAM, DO NOT SETTLE ON JOHN WAYNE'S RANCH, DO NOT CLEAR THE PROCESSING AREA, TAKE PAPERS BACK TO 'START.' "**

*The Vietnam War is still with us in the form of hapless refugees.*

6/13/75

6/2/75

**"ASSASSINATE? OH, PLEASE DON'T USE THAT AWFUL WORD! SAY, RATHER, WE ACT WITH EXTREME PREJUDICE . . ."**

*The CIA, we are told, has been trying to assassinate Castro of Cuba for a good many years and, failing that, has indulged in some bizarre plots to discredit him.*

11/24/75

**"ER . . . IT'S SUPPOSED TO SUCK YOUR BRAINS OUT, AND THEN I TAKE THEM BACK TO WASHINGTON, AND . . ."**

9/18/75

**"EASY WITH THAT STUFF—ONE DROP CAN KILL 500,000 PEOPLE!"**

*When not engaged in Castro games, the agency involves itself developing exotic weapons, poisons and other devices best kept within the plots of James Bond movies.*

10/24/75

**"YOUR AUNT MURIEL IS SICK AND WISHES YOU'D WRITE . . . A BILL . . . YOUR NO-GOOD KID ON THE EUROPE TOUR WANTS MONEY . . . ANOTHER BILL . . . POSTCARD FROM THE FIGBYS IN HAWAII . . . JUNK . . ."**

*The CIA also reserves to itself the right to open and read your mail.*

6/22/75

**"BE THANKFUL, COMRADE, WE DON'T LIVE WITH A GOVERNMENT WHICH SPIES ON PEOPLE, PLANS ASSASSINATIONS, BUGS OFFICES, TAPS TELEPHONES, LIES TO US . . ."**

6/30/75

*Indira Gandhi moves against her political opponents.*

7/22/75

**"THIS SHOULD BE EASY ENOUGH—
JUST MENTION 'DETENTE' AND HE'LL SIGN ANYTHING!"**

*Russia is eager for wheat, the United States too eager for détente.*

8/4/75

NEVILLE CHAMBERLAIN, 1975

7/25/75

THE THIRTEEN CENT STAMP IS COMING!
THE THIRTEEN CENT STAMP IS COMING!
LETTER CARRIERS CONTRACT
U.S. MAIL
THEY WERE GOING TO STRIKE— BUT WHO'D NOTICE?

7/27/75

THE BLACK MAN'S BURDEN

9/12/75

**"900 FEET AND LEVEL, SKIPPER—SAY, DID WE BRING THAT GO-GO DANCER IN FROM THE FOREDECK?"**

*A Navy submarine skipper was relieved of his command after a go-go dancer performed topless on the ship's deck as it sailed out of Port Canaveral, Florida.*

9/15/75

**"WE GOT A LITTLE BEHIND WITH OUR SOCIAL SECURITY OVERPAYMENT REPAYMENT PAYMENTS . . ."**

*Hundreds of millions of dollars are paid out in error as a computer system at the Social Security Administration goes on the fritz.*

9/16/75

**"I'M GETTING A LOT OF CALLS LIKE THIS— IT SEEMS TO BE SOMETHING THAT'S GOING AROUND!"**

10/2/75

**THEREFORE, NEVER SEND TO KNOW**
**FOR WHOM THE BELL TOLLS. IT TOLLS FOR THEE.**

*Franco of Spain is dead.*

10/20/75

**"MR. FORD WAS WONDERING IF YOU WOULD LIKE TO BUY A PUPPY . . ."**

*The Fords' golden retriever, Liberty, has puppies.*

9/24/75

**"I DON'T THINK SHE'LL TRY ANYTHING—SHE SAYS SHE'S BEEN CLEARED BY THE SECRET SERVICE!"**

*San Francisco—a dowdy little lady, Sara Jane Moore, gets close enough to take a shot at President Ford.*

9/25/75

**THE PRESIDENT, 1976**

*The country seems to have more than enough maniacs to go round, so . . .*

10/1/75

**"OK, THREE PACES TO THE REAR—AND, PLEASE, NO SEX-ROLE TALK!"**

*A visit from Emperor Hirohito of Japan.*

11/14/75

"A CONSERVATIVE CHOICE WILL GIVE YOU TROUBLE IN THE SENATE, A LIBERAL CHOICE WILL GIVE YOU TROUBLE FROM REAGAN—AND IF YOU DON'T CHOOSE A WOMAN, I'LL MAKE YOUR LIFE HELL!"

10/21/75

**"GET OUTA HERE! LIKE I KEEP TELLIN' YOU, THE MONEY SHOULD ARRIVE FROM MY RICH UNCLE ANY TIME NOW!"**

*New York plunges deeper into debt and waits for relief from Washington.*

10/29/75

**"CLASS! THAT'S ONE THING THEY CAN'T TAKE AWAY FROM US NEW YORKERS—OUR CLASS!"**

11/11/75

"HE FOLLOWED US HOME—CAN WE KEEP HIM?"

10/30/75

**"THEY WON'T ALLOW US TO JOIN HERE—LET'S GO OVER TO THE LITTLE LEAGUE AND SEE IF THEY'LL LET US IN THERE!"**

*The girls were admitted to the little leagues, but antisexism proved to be a one-way street. The Girl Scouts refused to allow boys to join.*

11/2/75

**"THE SUPREME COURT SAYS YOU MAY PADDLE A STUDENT, MISS PERKINS—SO, GO AHEAD AND PADDLE HIM"**

11/17/75

*Congress is uneasy with the powers of Henry Kissinger, but nobody really wants to tie any bells on a cat that nasty.*

8/5/75

**"JUST BECAUSE INDIRA GANDHI GETS AWAY WITH JAILING THE OPPOSITION, STOPPING THE MEDIA, CHANGING THE LAW, AND FORGIVING HERSELF IS NO REASON TO KICK THE POOR DOG!"**

*Meanwhile, back at San Clemente . . .*

8/22/75

**RICHARD IN WONDERLAND**

*In his first public statement since his resignation, Nixon gives a six-hour deposition at San Clemente to members of a grand jury investigating the Watergate case. He seems to have changed little.*

11/19/75

**"A WAR! THAT'S WHAT THE IMMORAL AMERICAN PEOPLE NEED! GIVE 'EM BACK A SENSE OF PURPOSE! I'LL COME BACK AND LEAD THEM! THEY LOVE ME . . . ARGLE BARGLE DRIBBLE BURBLE . . ."**

*"We [Americans] are so cynical, so disbelieving," says ex-President Nixon, "it may take the threat of invasion . . . to regain the sense of belief in our country and our need for strength. We are a compromised country at the moment." The man makes difficult listening.*

12/3/75

"LOOKS LIKE ISRAEL HAD A BAD DAY IN THE U.N. AGAIN!"

1/1/76

**THIS IS THE YEAR FOR A REVOLUTION . . .**

*Day One. America's Bicentennial Year.*

1/9/76

*Ronald Reagan decides he is the man for the Republican nomination.*

1/21/76

*Two thumbs and ten fingers.*

2/5/76

**CONCORDE GETS 16-MONTH TRIAL PERIOD—AND THEN . . .**

2/6/76

**"PROBABLY NO RELATION . . ."**

*Indira Gandhi continues with her familiar treatment for dissidents.*

2/11/76

**"WHY AREN'T YOU OUT THERE SAYING A LOT OF NEAT STUFF ABOUT PREMARITAL SEX AND ABORTION AND POT AND WOMEN'S RIGHTS . . . ?"**

*Reagan at a disadvantage.*

2/18/76

*The Lockheed Company begins losing orders for aircraft after it is discovered using bribery on a global scale to promote sales. Bribes may work where prayer fails . . .*

2/26/76

**"TAKE HIM HOME, PLEASE—HE'S BEGINNING TO MAKE ME NERVOUS!"**

*Nixon revisits China.*

3/5/76

**"CAN YOU HELP MR. CARTER, DOC? HIS SMILE IS STUCK . . ."**

*The Carter campaign moves along behind an obsequious, ingratiating smile.*

3/8/76

**"VERY TOUCHING OF YOU GUYS TO RUSH OVER SO QUICKLY TO SAY YOUR FAREWELLS . . ."**

*Senate Majority Leader Mike Mansfield retires. Senator Byrd wins the ensuing scuffle.*

3/23/76

**"HIT HIM AGAIN WITH THE DEODORANT!"**

*Congress works on legislation to put the Federal Election Commission back in business. Both Democrats and Republicans load the bill with self-serving amendments to benefit their special interests. A Tennessee senator with his integrity still intact terms it a "lousy, stinking, fraudulent bill."*

3/28/76

**"VE HAVE CONTINGENCY PLANS . . ."**

*A 12,000-man Cuban force intervenes in Angola. The administration in Washington is thought to be considering countering any further Cuban adventures with American action in this hemisphere. That raises awesome possibilities.*

3/31/76

**"HE'LL ACCEPT YOUR APOLOGY IN RETURN FOR ONE BILLION DOLLARS IN MILITARY AID, AND NO QUIBBLING ABOUT CYPRUS —YOU MAY NOW APPROACH AND KISS HIS FOOT!"**

*Left to himself, something he usually insists upon, Dr. Kissinger comes up with some strange arrangements.*

4/4/76

**"NOW WHAT??"**

*Just one thing after another—first the candidates, now this . . .*

4/7/76

*Faithful and beloved aides and associates grieve the passing of billionaire Howard Hughes.*

4/9/76

*Jimmy just keeps smiling out of both sides of his mouth.*

4/20/76

**"HARK! IT MUST BE SPRING—I HEAR SINGING . . ."**

*Good news from Jerry.*

4/27/76

*Kissinger tours Africa . . .*

5/5/76

5/22/76

**"DOCTOR KISSINGER, I PRESUME? . . ."**

*. . . and meets with Prime Minister Vorster of South Africa.*

4/28/76

**"CHARGE! SEND A GUNBOAT! WALK SOFTLY AND CARRY A BIG STICK! BULLY! BULLY!"**

*Reagan finds a campaign issue.*

5/13/76

**INTERIOR DEPARTMENT TO ALLOW VAST STRIP MINING IN WEST—News Item**

5/14/76

*As in all campaigns, the candidates eventually reach the CTP . . .*

5/16/76

**"COME ON OUT, JIMMY CARTER—
WE KNOW YOU'RE IN THERE!"**

*. . . and Jimmy continues smiling.*

5/25/76

**". . . ER . . . MY *OTHER* SECRETARY . . . MORE OF AN *AIDE*, REALLY . . . THIS WAY!"**

*Elizabeth Ray, the opportunistic "secretary who couldn't type," reveals that she has served as mistress to Senator Wayne Hays on a salary of $14,000 for a number of years.*

6/1/76

**"I'M SORRY, BRUCE, I KNOW YOU'RE A GOOD SECRETARY AND ALL THAT, BUT YOU'LL HAVE TO GO— WHAT WITH ALL THAT WAYNE HAYS FUSS . . ."**

*What would we do if politics and campaigns and other tedium were not relieved by this sort of thing now and then?*

6/6/76

6/13/76

**"I DON'T KNOW IF I SHOULD LAUGH OR CRY—
I'M THE ONLY CONGRESSMAN ON CAPITOL HILL
WHO DIDN'T GET MENTIONED IN ELIZABETH RAY'S BOOK!"**

6/10/76

**". . . AND, AH DECLARE, HERE'S GEORGEY WALLACE . . . AND GOOD OL' RICKY DALEY . . . AND WHO DO AH SEE COMIN'? . . . WHY, IT'S OL' SCOOPEY JACKSON!"**

*What is the explanation for the Southern habit of calling grown men by children's names? Later we will have a President with a name like this.*

6/24/76

*Ehrlichman, Haldeman write of their experiences in Nixon's White House. Everyone in for his piece of the action.*

7/2/76

7/4/76

*The nation's two hundredth.*

7/6/76

**A RAP ON THE KNUCKLES**

*International terrorists seize an Israeli airliner and hijack it to Entebbe airport in Uganda, where they are welcomed by President Idi Amin. Israeli commandos stage a magnificent raid on Entebbe to successfully free all but one of the hostages. Idi Amin is not amused.*

7/13/76

**METAMORPHOSIS**

*Returning morality to government is a Carter promise long before we ever hear of Bert Lance.*

7/8/76

**"THE ENVELOPE PLEASE . . ."**

*After the suitable amount of suspense, the announcement of the running mate.*

7/16/76

**COUNTRY BOYS**

*Jimmy has the Democratic nomination. Walter Mondale is his choice for Vice President.*

7/28/76

**"HAVE FAITH, MARTIN—IF MR. REAGAN ALLIES HIMSELF WITH A NO-GOOD, BUBBLE-HEAD EASTERN LIBERAL COMMUNIST PINKO, HE MUST HAVE A GOOD REASON!"**

*Shocking news back in Reagan country as he chooses a running mate.*

8/3/76

**". . . AND DER SOCKS. VE PROMISED ALSO DER SOCKS!"**

*Details surface of secret deals made around the world in the name of the United States by the well-known Dick and Henry team. This was an assistance deal for Iran.*

8/10/76

**"WE GOTTA GET SOME LEGISLATION GOING ON OPEN-CUT MINING BEFORE THIS WHOLE PLACE LOOKS LIKE AN EARTH-SCAPE!"**

*The Mars Lander takes a bite of the planet for examination in the search for signs of life.*

9/1/76

**"OH, THAT'S SPECIAL AGENT BRUCE OF THE INTERIOR DECORATION DIVISION . . . IF THAT HELPS YOUR MORALE AT ALL!"**

*Public examination of FBI abuses of power and authority has morale at a low ebb around that bureau according to reports.*

9/2/76

*Jimmy engages the tough issue of abortion with his usual straightforward, plain-speaking candor.*

9/5/76

**"PUT HIM DOWN FOR A NEW SET OF FAIRWAY WOODS, A TUNE-UP ON THE PORSCHE, AND MAYBE A QUICK WEEKEND IN VEGAS . . . OH, AND GIVE HIM A COUPLE OF ASPIRIN."**

*Many doctors have found by now that Medicaid is the mother lode.*

9/10/76

*Mao Tse-tung dies in Peking . . . and now the fun starts.*

9/15/76

*Riots, demonstrations and shootings—all the signs of imminent race war in southern Africa. Henry visits.*

9/26/76

**GREAT ISSUES OF 1976**

*President Ford has a wife who is outspoken on understanding her daughter's affairs, a son who claims to smoke grass, a Vice President who gives hecklers the finger and a political opponent who talks about lust to* Playboy *magazine. Such are the issues.*

**9/22/76**

*That's right. He talked to* Playboy *magazine about lusting after women in his heart.*

**10/10/76**

*The "joke" is, "I have been to Poland, and I can say that that country is not under Soviet domination!" He tells this during a televised debate with Jimmy Carter.*

10/17/76

**GREAT ISSUES OF 1976—PART TWO**

*While Gerald Ford tells Polish jokes, Earl Butz tells black jokes, but apart from arms for Israel, John Dean's book promotion and farm price supports there isn't much going on. Unless you want to bring up lust and* Playboy *magazine.*

10/12/76

**"ARE YOU REALLY SURE YOU WANT TO GET INTO THIS?"**

*Gene McCarthy considers getting into the act. But comedy was never his forte.*

11/3/76

*The winner.*

11/2/76

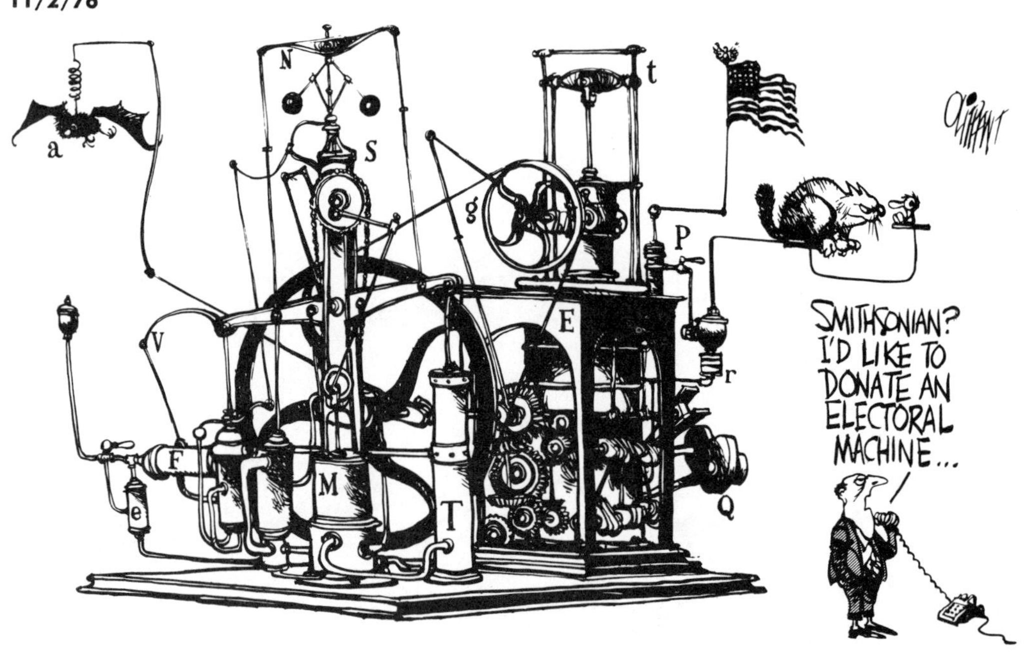


11/7/76

**"WHY ALWAYS AT THE STATION? DO Y'ALL HAVE TO ALWAYS DO THIS AT THE STATION?? HAVEN'T Y'ALL GOT A CHURCH TO GO TO?"**

*Jimmy goes home to Plains, Georgia, to receive the congratulations of the home folks. Some wondered why he always held these meetings at the railroad station.*

11/10/76

*Henry Kissinger prepares to leave office.*

**"TRANSITION IS HELL FOR MR. FORD, TOO, I WOULD IMAGINE . . ."**

11/19/76

**"YES, JIMMY, THE TRANSITION'S GOIN' ALONG FINE . . . THAT NICE MR. NESSEN INTRODUCED ME BRIEFLY TO THE BIG OL' HOUN' DOG THAT GOES WITH THE PLACE."**

*Jimmy hides out in Plains while his staff handles the transition details.*

3/12/69

**"THERE'S NOTHING ELSE HERE—I GUESS THAT WRAPS IT UP. . . ."**

*This cartoon was drawn for the* Denver Post *at the end of the inquiries by the Warren Commission into possibilities of conspiracy in the assassination of John Kennedy. The commission found no such possibility.*

11/28/76

**"DID YOU HEAR SOMETHING . . . ?"**

*The above was drawn for the* Washington Star *as inquiries reopened into the Kennedy assassination conspiracy. I later checked the drawings against each other to see how much I had remembered and forgotten. It was an interesting exercise in drawing from memory after almost eight years.*

11/30/76

**"THE REST OF YOU SECURE THE HALLS AND PLAYGROUND—BEGLEY, THAT'S YOUR CHAIR OVER THERE . . ."**

*Still smiling, Jimmy Carter announces that daughter Amy will attend public school in Washington. Amy does not smile as much as her father.*

12/1/76

*He's still trying to get at what he calls "his letters and tapes."*

12/7/76

**"COMPLIMENTS OF THE PEOPLE OF SOUTH KOREA, A SMALL DONATION TO AID YOU IN ANY INVESTIGATIONS YOU MAY BE UNDERTAKING . . ."**

*The House Ethics Committee conducts inquiries into the allegations that certain members of Congress had accepted large amounts of money and gifts from influence-buying South Korean diplomats and agents.*

12/19/76

*Most people turn their backs on the incredible Swine Flu Vaccination Campaign.*

1/5/77

*Consumers boycott coffee as the prices rise to prohibitive levels.*

1/11/77

**THE FIRST PERSON TO TRY IT**

*The Open Presidency.*

1/19/77

*Murderer Gary Gilmore demands that the state of Utah execute him rather than sentence him to life in prison. There is money and publicity to be made here, and the jackals move in. . . . The state of Utah eventually obliges Mr. Gilmore.*

1/20/77

**"GOOD MORNING, MR. PRESIDENT . . .
AND YOU CAN STOP SMILING NOW!"**

*Inauguration, and so to work.*

2/3/77

*Andrew Young is appointed U.S. Ambassador to the United Nations and takes off for Africa. At the same time, a black author, Alex Haley, is enjoying enormous success with his book* Roots, *an account of his search for his African forebears.*

2/6/77

"COME ON OUT AGAIN, MR. GROUNDHOG—I PLEDGE MY FIFTY-DOLLAR REBATE TOWARD GIVING YOU A DECENT FUNERAL!"

*The winter of early '77 is vile. Drought in the West, incredible cold in the East. To boost the economy, President Jimmy offers a program which includes a $50 rebate for all Americans. On Groundhog Day, the animal sees his shadow and goes back inside. It is all too much.*

2/10/77

*White supremacy and black-extremist activity in Rhodesia.*

2/13/77

**"PARDON ME, IS THIS THE OFFICE OF THE . . . NICE SHOT . . . HOUSE ASSASSINATIONS COMMITTEE?"**

2/18/77

**"DEAR PRESIDENT CARTER. I THOUGHT YOU WOULD BE PLEASED TO HEAR THAT HARRY AND I ARE NO LONGER LIVING IN SIN. WHEN I MENTIONED YOUR VIEWS ON THE SUBJECT, HARRY TOOK OFF . . ."**

*Beware a born-again President. He expresses his disapproval of government employees who are "living in sin," as he quaintly puts it.*

2/20/77

**THE CONGRESSMAN WHO PROPOSED A PAY CUT**

3/3/77

**MEANWHILE, OFF NEWFOUNDLAND: "MAYBE IN THE OFF-SEASON WE COULD GET WORK IN UGANDA!"**

*The seal-clubbers move in again for the kill off Newfoundland. Idi Amin has a reputation for having this done to people in Uganda.*

2/15/77

**". . . AND THIS IS FREDDIE, MR. PRESIDENT . . .
HE'D LIKE TO SAY HELLO, TOO. SAY 'HELLO,' FREDDIE . . ."**

*Jimmy Carter, President, announces he will go on the air and take calls and questions direct from the people . . .*

3/8/77

**"AS I WAS SAYING TO JIMMY—I CALL HIM JIMMY—WHEN WE SPOKE ON THE PHONE THE OTHER DAY, 'JIMMY,' I SAID. 'YES, FRED,' HE SAYS—HE CALLS ME FRED . . ."**

*. . . and, of course, everyone who gets through to talk to Jimmy is addressed accordingly.*

3/9/77

*New York residents express displeasure at the landing of the Concorde. Giscard d'Estaing of France expresses displeasure at the New Yorkers' objections. New Yorkers express their opinions of his displeasure, etc....*

3/10/77

3/13/77

**"YOU OUGHTA LAY OFF THAT COFFEE—**
**IT'S HIDEOUSLY EXPENSIVE!"**

*Enormous doses of saccharin may or may not cause cancer in laboratory animals. Evidence enough. It is decided to ban the substance.*

3/17/77

**"I SEE THIS MIRAGE—IT'S SMILING AT US . . . NO . . . NO, I'M WRONG, IT'S NOT SMILING AT US . . . IT'S *LEERING* AT US!"**

*Jimmy Carter decides that many water-conservation and dam-building programs proposed for the nation are unnecessary. Many of these dams are in the West. The West did not support Jimmy in his presidential election—not that there is any relationship between these points.*

3/20/77

"GET HER OUT OF SIGHT! THE PENTAGON MAY BE READY FOR WOMEN ON COMBAT SHIPS, BUT THE OLD MAN WILL NEVER BE!"

*What next!*

3/23/77

*Jimmy Carter speaks sternly on human rights in the USSR . . .*

3/30/77

**"DEAR MR. PRESIDENT. HAVE FOOT IN DOOR. PLEASE GO EASY ON THE DISSIDENT STATEMENTS OR I COULD LOSE FOOT. CYRUS."**

*. . . but making human rights for Russian dissidents a bargaining point in the SALT II disarmament negotiations has its disadvantages as far as Cyrus Vance, the negotiator, is concerned.*

3/31/77

"GIVE US ONE MORE ROUND, BARKEEP—WE, THE HOUSE ASSASSINATION COMMITTEE, HAVE DECIDED ON UNITY!"

4/3/77

**" 'SCUSE ME, SIR—I WAS WONDERING IF YOU'D CARE TO BE BORN AGAIN . . ."**

*A noble gesture. Jimmy is good at noble gestures.*

4/7/77



**"SOME MAY CALL IT AN OPEN ADMINISTRATION— I CALL IT PUSHY!"**

4/12/77

"WELL, IF YOU'RE NOT A FRENCHMAN DELIVERING MOROCCAN ARMS, AND YOU'RE NOT WITH THE CHINESE ARMS GROUP, AND YOU'RE NOT WITH THE REBEL-SUPPORTING CUBAN CONTINGENT FROM ANGOLA, WHAT ON EARTH ARE YOU DOING HERE?"

*Everyone into Zaire!*

4/13/77

**"WHAT FISH?"**

*The Jimmy administration moves against illegal fishing activities by Russian trawlers.*

4/17/77

**"YOU LOSE—START AGAIN!"**

*Same as last year. And the year before. And the year before that . . .*

4/20/77

"WILL THERE BE ANY QUESTIONS?"

4/21/77

"YES, THIS IS YOUR MAILMAN . . . NO, I DON'T MAKE HOUSECALLS BUT IF YOU COME TO MY OFFICE YOU MAY PICK UP YOUR MAIL, BUT PLEASE DO CALL FOR AN APPOINTMENT . . ."

4/27/77

**"WE COULD HAVE GONE TO CALIFORNIA! WE COULD HAVE GONE TO ARIZONA! BUT, OH, NO! YOU HAVE TO RETIRE TO DADE COUNTY, FLORIDA!"**

*Anita Bryant, gospel singer and TV orange juice salesperson, claiming that homosexuals are holding too many important positions of public trust, forces a special election in Dade County, Florida, to repeal the laws protecting homosexuals.*

6/9/77

*And in the election results, Bryant prevails.*

6/29/77

**"RIOT CONTROL HAS CHANGED A LOT SINCE THE GOOD OLD NINETEEN SIXTIES, HASN'T IT?"**

*Gays demonstrate for their rights in San Francisco.*

5/3/77

**"CORRECT! CONTESTANT NIXON, YOU NOW HAVE THREE HUNDRED AND SIXTY THOUSAND DOLLARS!!—FOR ANOTHER FIVE HUNDRED DOLLARS, ANSWER THIS QUESTION . . ."**

*Television personality David Frost arranges for a series of TV interviews with Richard Nixon. Nixon's fee is $600,000. Who says crime doesn't pay?*

5/5/77

**"DADDY BROKE MR. NIXON!"**

*The sight of the man who used to be President, telling his old lies all over again and telling some new ones as well, and all for money, does not sit well with most of the populace. The greatest service the interviews perform is to refresh our memory as to the sort of man Nixon is. And this is too soon for many of us.*

5/29/77

*"I am not a crook!" he once said.*

5/8/77

**WARNING: ANDREW YOUNG, THE CRAZED TOE-STOMPER, IS STILL AT LARGE**

*Andrew Young has not yet found his diplomatic balance.*

5/13/77

"FIRST THE GOOD NEWS . . . WHEN YOU WERE A BOY YOUR UNCLE FRANKLIN D. SET UP A TRUST FUND FOR YOUR RETIREMENT YEARS. THE BAD NEWS IS SOME SCOUNDREL SEEMS TO HAVE SPENT IT ALL!"

5/17/77

*Another Jimmy gesture.*

5/19/77

"YOU'LL HAVE TO PREACH A LITTLE LOUDER TO THIS BUNCH!"

5/22/77

**"IN *THAT*!!??"**

*Fiftieth anniversary of Lindbergh's crossing of the Atlantic.*

5/27/77

**"WELL, WELL, WELL . . . LOOK WHAT *I* FOUND!"**

*He criticized Gerald Ford's use of it during his campaign. Then he discovered what fun it could be . . .*

6/2/77

**"OK, NOW . . . WHO WANTS A SOUTH-AMERICAN FLAVOR? . . . AN' WHO WANTS A CUBAN? . . . AN' WHO WANTS A GOODOLBOY? . . . AN' A SOVIET? . . . AN' A . . ."**

*Whatever flavor you want . . .*

6/10/77

**"HEY, JIMMY—YOU GET RID OF THAT BIG OL' DINOSAUR YET?"**

*As part of his energy program, Jimmy Carter tries for legislation to outlaw the "gas-guzzler" automobile.*

6/28/77

THE COUPLE UPSTAIRS

7/1/77

*Unexpectedly, Carter shoots down plans for the controversial B-1 Bomber, proposed replacement for the aging B-52.*

7/7/77

**"EUREKA!"**

*Revolutionary, clean, more humane, a bomb that kills but leaves buildings intact!*

7/10/77

**ANDY YOUNG MAY GET HIS OWN TALK SHOW, TV SOURCES SAY . . .**

*And now . . . he-e-e-ere's Andy!*

7/15/77

*More fun in Fun City. . . . Lightning strikes and we have the Great New York Blackout.*

7/19/77

**"COME BACK TOMORROW AND TRY FOR A DECISION—
WE'RE BEING WISHY-WASHY TODAY!"**

*Decisions, decisions, decisions . . .*

7/24/77

**"DEAR MR. CARTER. I HEARD SOMEWHERE
THAT YOU HAVE AN INTEREST IN HUMAN RIGHTS . . ."**

8/3/77

**"WE'LL HAVE TO CALL OFF OPERATION MIND-CONTROL— THERE'S NOTHING HERE!"**

*More revelations of fantastic CIA voyages into control of the human mind.*

7/21/77

**"THERE, THERE! TAKE YOUR TIME SELLING THEM, BERT—CONGRESS JUST TOLD ME THEY REALIZE THIS ETHICS NONSENSE CAN GET WAY OUT OF HAND!"**

*Good ol' buddy Bert Lance is Jimmy Carter's appointee to be director of the Office of Management and Budget. This poses some problems when it comes time for confirmation in Congress. Some problems, but nothing serious . . .*

8/11/77

**"NOT RIGHT NOW, JIMMY—I'M BUSY DIRECTING THE MANAGEMENT AND BUDGET . . . MY MANAGEMENT AND MY BUDGET!"**

*. . . nothing very serious.*

8/12/77

*Carter takes a flier with his Panama Canal Treaty, the proposal to turn over eventual control of the waterway to Panama.*

8/14/77

**"MISS HOCKLEY, TAKE A POSTCARD . . ."**

8/16/77

**TEX JAWORSKI'S BACK IN TOWN**

*Leon Jaworski, of Watergate fame, comes back to head an inquiry into South Korean influence-buying in Congress.*

8/19/77

*Infamous New York killer known as Son of Sam is apprehended. The usual appalling sideshow develops.*

8/21/77

*The treaty isn't selling well . . .*

8/23/77

**"NO, WE CERTAINLY DIDN'T ASK THE SAME COLLATERAL FROM BERT LANCE . . . WHY DO YOU ASK?"**

*The Bert Lance confirmation is not selling well, either. Apparently ol' Bert could raise a loan for a million or so more easily than the ordinary citizen could raise a loan for a hundred.*

8/24/77

*The President nominates a stern, quiet and dignified federal judge from Alabama as the new FBI director.*

8/25/77

**"FUNNY—I FEEL LIKE I HAVEN'T EATEN A THING!"**

*Cyrus Vance visits China to explain Carter's positions on things like Taiwan and the administration's interest in continuing good relations with the People's Republic and nothing much else.*

8/26/77

**"SO!! HIDING IN HERE TRYING TO AVOID A HEART ATTACK, HUH? WE'LL SEE ABOUT THAT!"**

8/28/77

**"I'M CALLING FOR VOLUNTEERS— WHO'LL FOLLOW ME TO PANAMA?"**

*The jingoists are vocal in defense of the Panama Canal. Anything physical will have to be done by much younger men, as it was in Vietnam.*

**8/30/77**

**"WE INTERRUPT THIS MUGGING MOMENTARILY WHILE WE PAUSE FOR A COMMERCIAL!"**

*An election for mayor of New York with street-crime control a major issue.*

**9/7/77**

Dear Gordon Liddy
Congratulations on your release!!
Now, Gordon, knowing what a hot-head
you are I don't want you hanging
around here thinking I owe you
something just because you may think
I got off Scott-free. I must say that
I'm disappointed you copped out and took
that Paupers Oath instead of hanging
tough as I would have done. But
as I said to David (Frost) the other
day if it hadn't been for Martha
Mitchell (God rest her) none of this
have happened in the first
done any time in

OLIPHANT

*Gordon Liddy, the Watergate conspirator who refused to testify, is released from prison after serving more than fifty-two months.*

**9/4/77**

*Bert Lance has been told by Jimmy Carter, "Bert, I'm proud of you!" So Bert stays around.*

**9/11/77**

**"IT'S A MESSAGE FOR YOU, BERT, FROM THE BANKING COMMUNITY . . . OR MAYBE IT'S FOR ME, I CAN'T REALLY TELL . . . OR MAYBE FOR BOTH OF US . . ."**

*Bert the Banker is getting irate messages from outside. They also want Bert to go away. But Bert still sticks around.*

9/13/77

*Another wonderful suggestion from the Jimmy administration. Local youngsters will be recruited to move around the neighborhoods and report on energy waste by householders.*

9/15/77

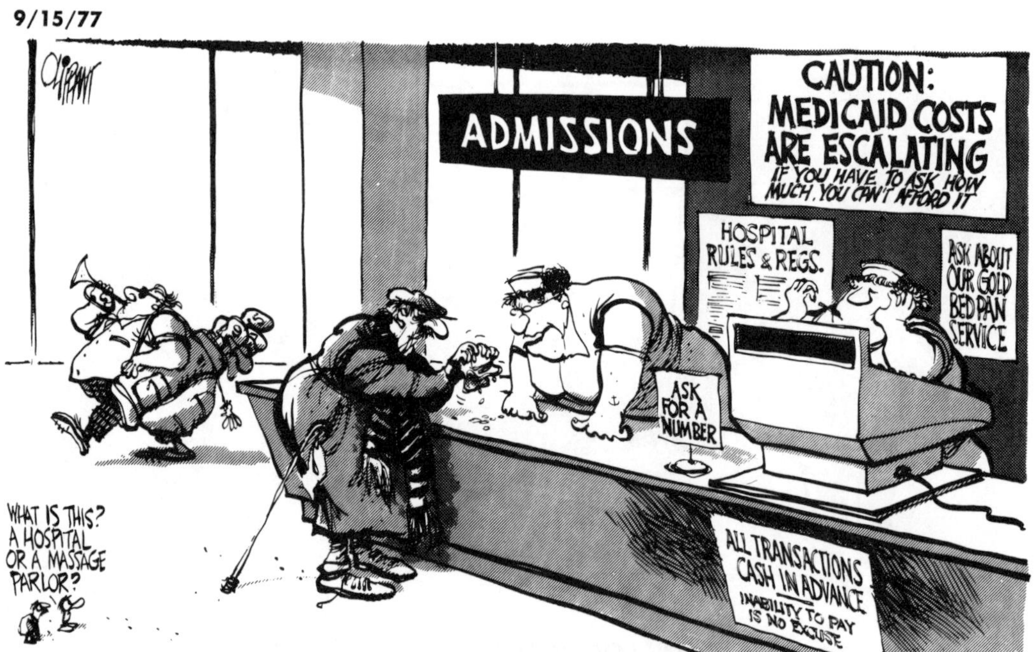


**"OH, GOODIE!! THAT AND YOUR MEDICAID CARD WILL GET YOU FORTY-FIVE MINUTES OF PRIME CARE— WILL YOU TAKE IT STANDING UP, IN A CHAIR, OR IN BED FOR FIFTY CENTS EXTRA?"**

9/20/77

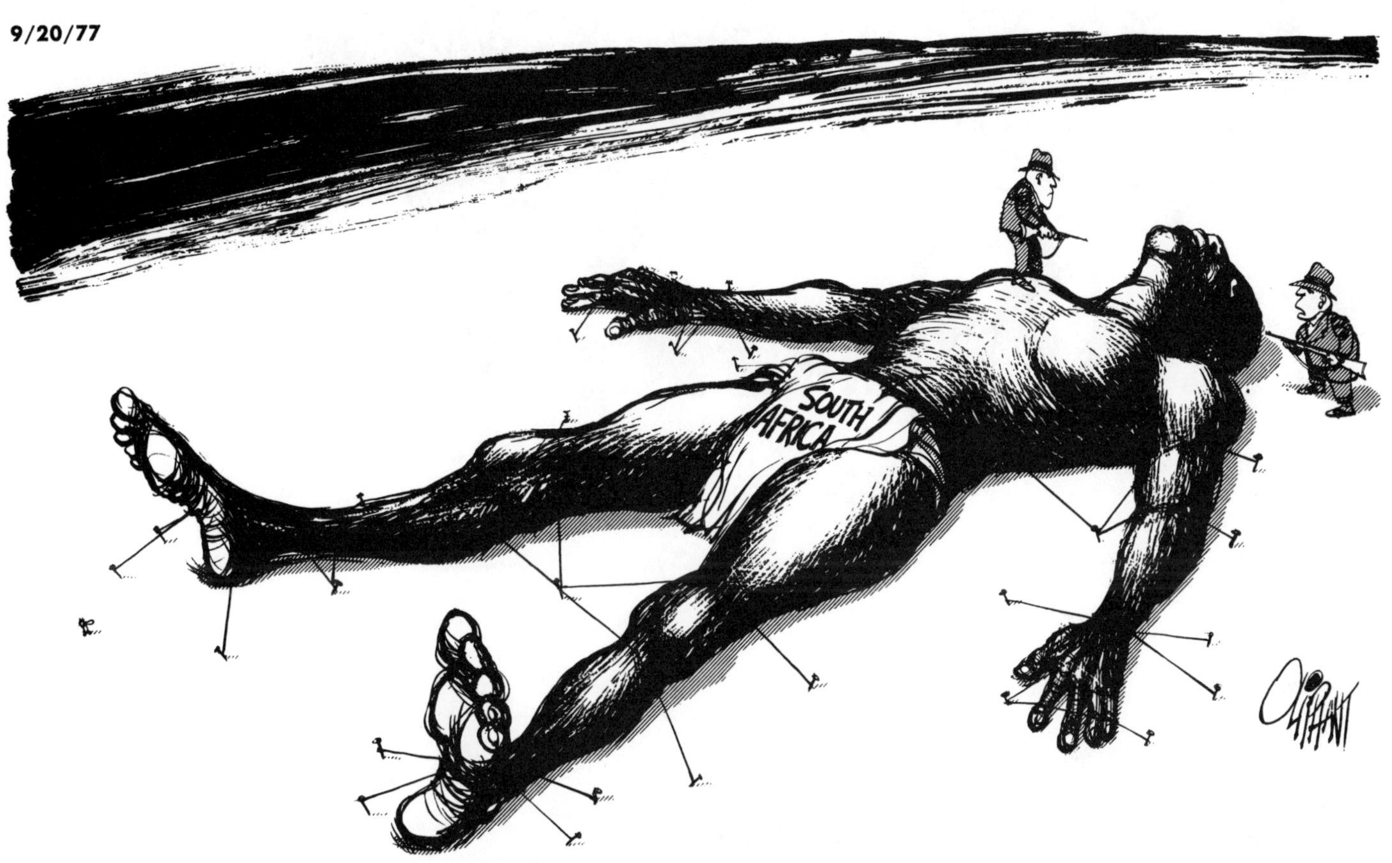


**"NOW, BEHAVE YOURSELF, OR WE'LL BE FORCED TO HAVE YOU DIE OF A HUNGER STRIKE!"**

*Stephen Biko, an educated and respected black leader in South Africa, dies in prison supposedly of the effects of a hunger strike. Later he is found to have suffered multiple injuries.*

**9/21/77**

*Vision trouble. Bert Lance is still hanging around . . .*

**9/22/77**

*. . . until, much to the regret of the Jimmy administration, he suddenly leaves.*

9/22/77

*In the Bakke case in California, white student Allan Bakke was twice turned down for admission to medical school although his grades were higher than some of the minorities who were admitted over him. Bakke sues, claiming this is a racial-quota system. Affirmative Action defended the minority students' position.*

9/28/77

**"YOU HAD TO ASK, DIDN'T YOU!—'236 DOLLARS TRANSATLANTIC LONDON–NEW YORK ROUND TRIP?' HE SAYS!—'DON'T YOU HAVE ANYTHING CHEAPER THAN THAT?' HE SAYS . . ."**

*Freddie Laker, British entrepreneur, offers greatly reduced fares on no-frills flights to England.*

9/29/77

**"IT'S WORSE THAN I THOUGHT—WE SEEM TO HAVE A KOREAN EPIDEMIC!"**

*The South Korean influence-buyers will stop at nothing.*

*When Brezhnev dances, everyone dances.*

10/5/77

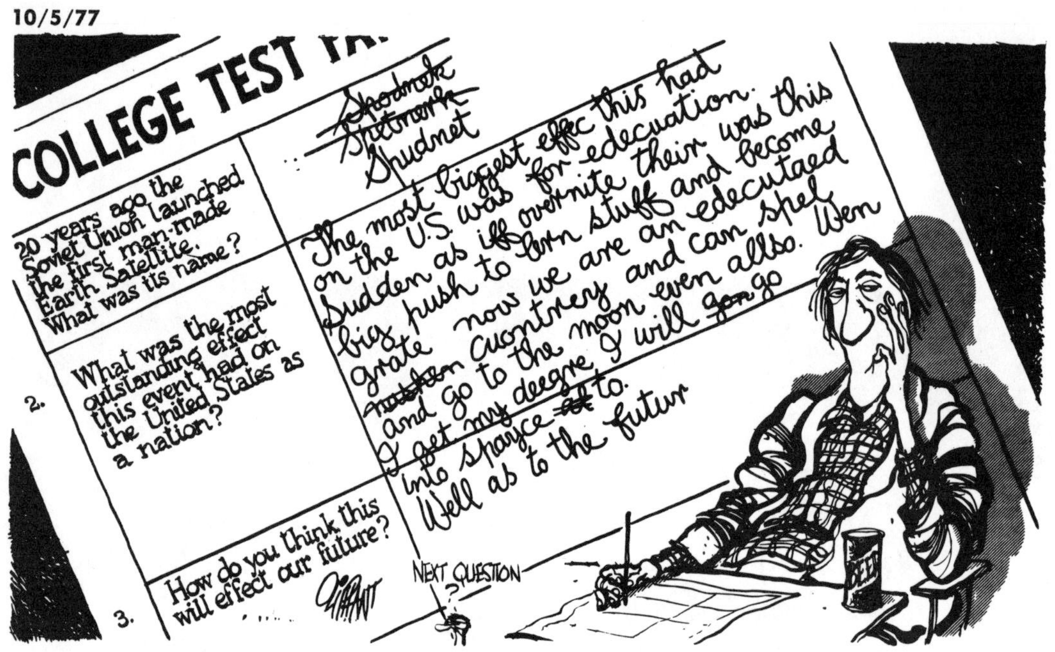


*The twentieth anniversary of the first Sputnik flight. Note that in the third question the educators also have trouble with thier speling.*

10/6/77

**KING BYRD OF THE SENATE PRESENTS SALOME WITH THE HEAD OF JOHN THE CONSUMER . . .**

*Natural-gas deregulation is approved in the Senate.*

10/14/77

*Some say that officers' training at West Point lacks a sense of humor. Ha! Ha! says the Army.*

10/26/77

**"SEE? WE SIMPLY TAKE AWAY HIS NEWSPAPER AND HE'S DOCILE AS A LAMB!"**

*Vorster of South Africa, forever the optimist . . .*

10/30/77

"TELL YOU WHAT I'M GONNA DO—YOU GIVE ME A BOTTLE OF YOUR BEST MUSCATEL, AND THE MOMENT MY BROTHER IS ELECTED PRESIDENT, I SHALL ENDORSE IT!"

*Billy Carter, brother to the President, endorses his own brand of beer.*

11/2/77

"REMEMBER HOW WE USED TO LAUGH WHEN OL' JERRY FORD WOULD GO AROUND BASHING HIS HEAD INTO EVERYTHING?"

11/8/77

"... HAPPY BIRTHDAY TO YOU! NOW, BLOW OUT THE CANDLE, CUT THE CAKE AND MAKE A WISH. YOU MUST THEN REPORT THE WISH TO THE PEOPLE'S MINISTRY OF WISH CONTROL!"

*For the U.S.S.R., an anniversary.*

11/23/77

**"OH, HI, DEAR! COME ON IN AND TELL US ABOUT THE WOMEN'S CONVENTION . . ."**

*A huge convention of women activists in Houston stirs up a deal of dissension—mainly among the participants.*

12/17/77

**BUSINESSMEN'S LUNCH**

*Born-again President Jimmy is horrified at the thought of the deductible three-martini lunch.*

12/20/77

*Coming up to Christmas, Israel is responding to Egypt's amazing peace initiatives. If only the third wise man would shut up.*

**12/25/77**

**"LORD SAVE US, HARRY—
NOW THEY'VE GOT THEIR OWN NAVY!"**

*The New Navy.*

**12/31/77**

*President Jimmy's first overseas trip. He arrives in Poland and is hopelessly misinterpreted by his State Department-approved interpreter. The embarrassment is compounded when he starts telling American jokes. Oh, well, three more years . . .*